The Deer in Your Garden

Poems by
Thomas Rankin

Published by Verdant Valley Books,
an imprint of Transreal Books

First Edition

Paperback ISBN: 978-1-940948-56-0
Ebook ISBN: 978-1-940948-57-7

Photograghs © Barbara P. Ash 2024

For Ann, Tia, Barbara, and Terry

Contents

The Deer in Your Garden

All day laboring
with water and soil
and sun you've cultivated
joys from unseen roots
now at evening
you retire inside
when many images of the mind
come unmoored they join
your day's work their likenesses

your flourishing kin outside
wrote the journals of their love
giving of themselves to the story
your father's boutonniere
your mother's bouquet
your sister's corsage

even your own primrose if any
held in perfection for a moment

bound all together in a still life
album of twilight through your window
and it seems that evening
has drawn it to completion
grafted to the store of immortelles
in the cold frame of your dreams

look now through the pane
your breath is the weight
of its own faint mist no more
gentle on the window glass

next you see
moving gingerly among the leaves
one tiny-hooved creature
complicating the vision
the mascot of the dreamers
craving nourishment
hunger not easily subdued
nibbling off morsels of old fancies
blossoms holding more than memories

love grace and sympathy
what drew her forebears together
in one song of life
bring this fawn to dine alone.

Rehearsal

Memory is pacing its trail in the woods
back and forth as though on all new ground
not divining how it might have done
so many frail deeds in dappled light
pieces of itself in sunshine clear
as the day it struck a patch of courage
the first time ever
which once lucid fades again
reined back neatly in the half-hitches
stalled in the shadows
till the steed returns among its gaits.

Meteorology

Here's a calm surface on the ocean
showing all the clouds
where we need not lift our eyes,
then one bird reflected from above
plunging after what it comes to be,
like passing through a mirror
of unshattered glass;
clouds watching also
the steady pulse of the lighthouse beam.
We talk softly, ears perked up for rain.

Weathering

If ever my hands pour forth water,
let it seem like rain.
Let it not be traced to me
but to the lead lining in the clouds.
Now is when it will be good to stand
outside the circle
storm drought storm drought storm
though we're born in the middle of it,
yes and we are all at sea
so that the horizon falls
when the ocean rocks us back,
rising up again
as we reel forward,
and wonder can we fathom
the deluge slipping through our fingers?

❀

Midwinter

The rain angles down
like a cold moist breath
of one who has been too long
on the streets of gold above.
The soul's contending emissaries
rush together, a ferocious wind,
trapping in their wars
all who live nearby.

What becomes of them?
Scattering hailstones,
steps leading away from the weather,
shutting of hurricane doors.

Still, each one goes its own way,
with so many ways
thrown into the world,
they will make their way

like the name given to them at birth.
They answer to it,
in time they speak it,
theirs and yet not theirs.

Bottled

To anyone who has yet to be

May you find this photograph in peace
Silence resting on its laurels
Before breezes unlock an archive
Another time

Solitude pondering all that it
Has accomplished with its thoughts alone
Through the desiccating wind
Separating our ages

The sea captains lamenting
No one would remember us
There was no vessel to convey us
It had sailed with the old century

While the ocean stayed behind for shelter
Saving this portrait of still morning
I had just tried on the hat seen here
Mentioned in the prophecies though not by name.

❄

Uncharted

There were golden days that never found
place on calendars or in journals,
spaces claimed by the dates of battles
we never fought in though
we'd heard their stories.

Golden days all unselfconscious
never sought to call themselves into being,
knowing only when they breathed and glowed,

wishing only to be peopled by quiet
joyous creatures and to find
anonymous others like themselves.

✦

Title

Sundry balladeers
pressing old
labels on the land
taking each other's
names as their own

down for centuries
reaching toward infinity
each anthem stepping closer
to uncreation.

Can we be there yet
when we're here already?

But the annals hail
us on our journey
luring us to browse

on the road to what becomes
our destiny
away in the distance.

Think of the languages
this story has been told in.

❖

Archaeology

Was there ever a window
where I'm standing now
breathing in the boundless air
this is an old spot old as the earth
perhaps a square of glass
looking like the promise
of another world come true
held up then by a tower
before that a waterway
for ancient vessels
their hulls of mahogany
inspiring chanties
the air in the hold
which side was it on
watching itself unknowingly
and after the fall
inside and outside
rushing together again.

Emblazoned

Where enlightenment has left a scar
shining like hot meteors
frozen in mid-fall
rehearsing battles in empty space
comets posing still in their mad rush

while here below shorebirds predecease
those who sing of them
and of their hatchlings
almost reaching them twice in an age
time takes its own self and them

the sea remembers me now
crested to the nines
heraldic shadow of its one face
making me feel worth my salt

water is my flesh and blood
I gather the earth in my embrace
recollecting parallels.

Perfect

Look how the sun lifts itself
overhead in the morning
it has grown strong with repetition

hear the birds singing that lovely song
they learned from someone
who must have led them ten thousand hours
else how could they sing without the score
breeze comes gently with an angel's touch
like one that surprises wrestling man
else how could the air
take a shape like this

days are talking to themselves
telling these stories
nights too and we overhear

we want them to be happy
we do all we can.

*

Beaming

Only tell me we shall meet again
and my mind will soar with joy
from this day and age
to a hundred other times
none like the present,

inseparable light bodies,
neither of us knowing bounds,
driven by the gen we thirsted for,
peering in a thousand window panes
where the silver and the pearls are laid,
each of them our very own,

then after every future,
your contemporary once again,
racing with the thought of you,
making the way home in spirit,
home to our fixed star.

❋

Clam Sauce

I've been wanting to tell you.
Have I done something?
Not a single thing.
Only I found out
the price of canned clams
is going way up
in the stores.
Thought you ought to know.
It's just the way of the world,
and nothing to do with us.
Sure am glad of that.
I would never want to be a clam.
The cost is too high;
then to be dumped over noodles
in a saucepan, minced
with onion, smashed with garlic,
doctored too with anesthetic wine
poured over my head
if the chef can find it.
No, I'd never want to be a clam,
not at any price.
Know what I'm saying?

❖

One of the Humors

Why do the stars fade
when the morning comes

still no place to rest while minds conspire
what names to murmur

chipping hearts away
leaving one honed arrow point to fly

past a ferocious whisper
frozen in the air

hoping some new moon
puzzles out one of its humors

not far from here in another time
someone took breath air was easy then

this was someone who
breathed as we might now

the quality of silence
unique to this place

drifting all unseen from ancient trees
to untroubled ears

I look around you seeing
those old times again

but rippling with sounds
of a small stream purling among obstructions

and I listen only to water
for which is more to be feared

the fate of the river or
the fate of its name.

Candlestick by Riverside

Small boy looking down
a short way to the ground,
coral corduroys keenly
creased like spiraling
designer candle, cap a
red flame on young wick,
burning to grow long shadows.

Sierra Yard at Night

Lunar light throws shadow
near dark as solid form,
bush, stark black, no nuance.

Colorless moonbeams light
wee grassblade silhouettes,
spikes on the meadow's floor.

Snakes who would bask by day
now languish underleaf,
moods cold as very night.

Cats' eyes in the darkness
can follow even the
thinnest flicker of ghost.

A horse stalks past, having
broken from the corral,
with silence on its trail.

❈

The Dawn Itself Is Quiet

The dawn itself is quiet. Hear the sound
Of wood fires crackling, pushing off the cold
As day begins and earth goes turning round.

Or were those wood fires, was that not the sound
Of rifles cracking, making soldiers bold?
The dawn itself is quiet. Hear the sound

Of marching toward the camp on frozen ground,
The boots of men returning to their hold
As day begins and earth goes turning round.

They whisper of the enemy they found
Surprised in sleep, and from their sleep cajoled.
The dawn itself is quiet. Hear the sound

Of bugles blowing reveille, and bound
To anger soldiers in their blankets rolled
As day begins and earth goes turning round.

They waken neither victors homeward bound,
Nor vanquished in their blankets keeping cold.
The dawn itself is quiet. Hear the sound
As day begins and earth goes turning round.

❖

Good Night Again

If we've ever missed a word
we may ask again
though with an answer
we disremember

till we know each other's names
middle and last from the very first
there is no leaving one off the roll
of the lifetime we stay on to learn

while the tree stretches its limbs
then settles in for a night
with the squirrels in their nests

let the wind blow where it may
through eternity's
departures without ending.

Artists at Work

There's a place I love to stand
to find the street perspective,
an angle on the people,
and on the bridge that reaches
across the stream that gives
this town its name. A path
stretches past the bridge
into the forest. Light
shows this world, and craft
shows the way beyond.

Come with me now and bring
a pencil or a brush,
come let us work our trade,
as we draw from life.

❂

Blood, Sweat and Tears

These three share one element,
that which gives life pungency,
and makes it glisten.

Blood is the eldest,
furnishing a home,
sweat, our labor's firstborn fruit,
sometimes blossoming in tears,
tears we savor now and then,
all that we can do wherewith.

Oh and these three
have one other thing
in common,
they have dwelt in the same house
in their finest hour.

Back Story

I keep waking up in places
where I never went to sleep.
The people there are mostly
kind to me. Though apparently
we've never met before,
all seem to have memorized
about me things I don't recall.
Lost dreams? Now I wonder
if the color of some
gone everyman's hair was
my dark shade of brown.
Not that, not that, they answer,
and if you weren't so young
in our ways, you'd never ask.
Some day you're going to learn.

And so against that day,
they teach me all their skills;
they explain their politics;
they tell me all their jokes;

they invite me to their festivals,
showing me their intricate
dance steps, carefully saving
our ballroom tickets in scrapbooks
to read later in armchairs.

These are the ways of another sleep,
I tell myself, though strangely,
I've grown to love these strangers.
Still, I miss my proper time
and place. To keep my wits,
I keep repeating, My eyes
will open soon, back home
where I nodded off with
my cat of many calendars.

That was last week.
Still not soon enough.
It feels like years. I
call to myself as a mantra,
Wake up, wake up,
I must wake up.

What if I did? Maybe I'm
still caught, and if I am,
whose dream is this?
Could I have dreamed
all these happenings in
an hour, or have I aged?

I am too small a basket
for all their eggs. *Oh no,*
they croon, *you will do fine.*
Stay here. They kiss their hands
to me and fade. *But wait,*
I call, *you haven't felt*
of my shoes yet, have you?
Which of us walks?
Then I wake up somewhere else.

❖

Faraway Song

The time and place I heard,
distant as the song itself,
where all such things belong,
or so we think –
late one night, a tiny
house in a valley, dark
with shadow, far from here,
however you choose to go.

The tune itself, though – airwaves
brought it home. It stayed
warm and steady on the hearth.
It flows yet in memory
from that still place, made thus
of something more than distance;
and mightily declares
a thoughtful joy.

This, my unwilling secret,
whose name I never knew,
the one I long to play
for you, had I the skill,
hails my spirit still.
Please you, in the silence,
may we listen for it now.

Hidden Assumptions

If I could stand
outside my house
and watch the lights
within, the sanctuary,
the fireflickers
and the love
all of it stands for
and the defiance of
the night from
which I observe —

yes, if I could.
I sometimes do
and meet myself
coming out to see
who is at the door.

Our Absent Friend

Her quiet, unobtrusive way
Drew notice every time –
Nordstrom bag, best brand of jeans,
Sneakers with the chambray spots,
Burberry Brit – she must have known
All eyes were on her; all could see
She'd been somewhere and had somewhere
To go. She sat on the bench and frowned
Often at her watch, a Guess.

Always when we came to town,
We spied her through the windshields
Of our cars, looking forward
To a glimpse, to our own conjectures.
One day she wasn't there. We mused.

The plan of her whole life was larger than this.
She intended to travel more places,

Learn many languages, invent some new
And varied devices, do much business,
Make more friends, meet more associates,
For we, mere passers-by, were not enough,
Despite her shows. She window-shopped
The best locales, and in between
Waited at the stops for transport.
What vehicle has taken her, and where?

One of Us

First it was too early,
then it was too late,
to teach us not to leap
or not to hesitate.
Both were in her lesson plans,
making us fret and fuss.
She drove us all distracted,
and she was one of us

We saw how ruthlessly
the mirror held her gaze,
and in our hungering hearts
no hopes were ever raised.
Spirits in desolation,
we'd nothing to discuss;
hence we crumbled quietly,
and she was one of us.

We scorned her paltry loyalty,
her false religion too.
Religion should envelop us,
so how could hers be true?
Her faith and ours had dwindled,
but when we'd left it thus,
she thought she saw the face of God,
and She was one of us.

Things We Did

We loved those old days
the magic of them
sent back then
just arriving now
waiting for them we ran out of time
there was no time soon
no home for the day itself
or the one pure note all creatures sing
above hearing range
just the sunshine we grew to cherish.

Airplane 2

As if God's hand smote
his perfect lenses
and shattered them, each
of us has an eye
trained on one of the
splinters of stained glass –
why we never blink
as we fly over
the wide world gazing
through tiny portholes
at immeasurable sky.

Artifacts

Read these bits of clay.
What an optimistic race,
as if they expected us,
trusting their judgment
would come down intact,
leaving ostrakons impressed
with the names of the banished,
making their owners shards of the tribe,
part of the excavation
proving the identities
that must go unmentioned
then and thenceforward,
their fame immortal now,
and the finding of their people
a legacy for inheritors
living in a distant time,
who piece together
and treasure an old story.

❖

Reprimanding

Reprimanding
him for not
compassionating
her affliction,
his ailing mother
inquired after
the whereabouts
of her woolen shawl.
He being young,
his soul; was tired,
his mind on Flaubert,
not on a shawl.
I watched the two,
suspecting somehow
indifferently,
between them lay
the universe's
discovery.

❖

Karaoke Talent

Sing to the wall
just you two
Sing to the window
not the crowd
Sing to the Bay
looking away
Sing to the bridge
that connects us
Sing to the ocean
and beyond
The genius
of the sea.

Birds of Passage

Are we not like those migrants,
winging here and there,
roosting on the boughs
of our destiny,
mindful to stay light?

Then they hurl us back
into searching air
for another branch
of purpose,
what must still be done,

each of us always
within call of the other,
holding to the sky
with just a quill;
we're of a feather.

⁂

Here She Comes!

The hours we waited
Amid straw since her brave
Departure at first light.
Huddled close, warm inside
Our circle (chilly the edge),
The sleepers annoyed
By the strident chirpers.

Yes, look now, there she is!
But no! But never mind.
And so we passed the time
Watchful in the nest
For the sight of our devoted,
A day's work in her bill!

And at the first real glimpse
My sisters and my brothers

Could not restrain themselves.
Skreee! cried some.

Wheee! cried others.
Hear hear! cried everyone.

Parliamentarians all.
Our gaping yellow beaks
Opened in debate.
Give us this food that we
May thrive and grow,
May sire another age

Or only that we cease
This longing now,
Safe in birdsleep
Before you fly again
Leaving us here to brood.

Two Homes

As a child I watched you swim away
looking back at us, going deep and
far into the ocean, wave by wave.
I was afraid for you and shouted,
Come back, come back, Father, stay on shore.
Mother said you were a strong athlete;
so I said, It's all right then, go on.
And you did until you swam too far
indeed; the waves took you all the way
to what we speak of as another
shore. Now only through the fog of night
can I call to you again. I feel
strength in your hand across my shoulder
as of a swimmer still robust, who
might be a part of this world yet, or
bearer of news from that other home.
I am calm until you rejoin the mist
before I can find my voice to ask,
Where you are, do I come to your dreams?

❂

Israel Moultrie in SF

This man on Sansome stands,
stands with his back to traffic,
facing the walkers to work,
and plays on amplified
guitar *Greensleeves* and *Fur Elisa*,
loosing beauty to the winds
of the highrise canyons.

A placard in Gothic proclaims
Israel Moultrie as his name,
and we like Israel's chosen
pass and receive his notes' blessing,
and offer into his instrument
case nickels and dollars and dimes
earned yet superfluous
to those who live on his smile.

❁

Findings

What was it I said then?
We'd stored all the apples
for a long season,
plenty of pumpkins,
cord of firewood. Even
the cats were arranged.

After eleven, hands
trailing off the coverlet,
you asked, was I ever
stirred by music? Yes, I
mumbled, started in
deliberation. The
words alone imported
something new, unheard of.

Outside the October wind,
gathering up spent leaves,
harvested their colors
from adjacent grounds.

On Time

What do we make of our years
striding over hills
padding through valleys
one of these our vision
of all there will be
days all of sunshine days all of rain
then a dream of stepping off
to a place of no mortality
our loved ones bowing their heads
as we pass can we exist then
simply in either world without end
let us make a trial of it here
bending to the work
take this hand and make of it
one five-pointed star
shining above the skies of winter
leave me the other
dusting stone with stars.

❁

Merlin Takes to the Woods

About him one of the oldest tales
was of his passion for Viviane,
whom the knowledge of his powers,
and not even all of these,
enabled to imprison him
in Broceliande Forest Tower.

What of his powers? He confounded
King Vortigern's magicians
with his barbèd prophecies –
son of an incubus and a nun.
The pillars of Stonehenge he caused
to fly Salisbury-way, and through
his magic was Arthur begot and born.

About the trees they say, again,
that it was under his own power
he sought them, being a warrior,
who had lost his reason in battle

but gained the gift of a seer
to guard in leaf-cave solitude.

But then there was Nimue,
the enchantress – he loved her too,
after a time, and through
the knowledge of his powers,
and not even all of these,
she buried him beneath a stone
which would not yield him a breath
(yet thus could he never breathe
his last). "O to be coiled
in brambles as in the wild," quoth he.
And lo, he was, from which
at times he still can be heard
speaking with the voice of a thorn.

Any Time

You were wondering about the year
you missed, about what we did,
gathered without you in our retreat
above the lake you could see through the spaces
here and there among the pines
when we stood outside the hall
on the deck that was wide enough
for all of us to fit. Well, you know
the same sun rose over us as over you
where you stayed that year and I'm sure
you felt the morning mist soon to dissipate
after the blossoms had sipped their fill.
And first the young people fed the horses,
which was as you taught them, then
we had juice and oatmeal in the hall,
and prayer, and afterwards the 10-year-olds
saddled up and rode along the trail
while the teenagers went hiking
clear to the rangers' lookout and back.

Next it seemed that in no time at all
the noon sun came to stop over us
just as I'm sure it did over you,
some miles to the east of us that year,
and the whole crowd came from everywhere they'd been
to the dining hall with the light streaming in
for onion stew and pumpernickel after grace,
and then we sang, but you know about that too,
for we sang the numbers that we learned from you.

On the day I'm thinking of, one of the older
women picked three of our teenagers
to lead us all in songs of their choice,
songs of course that everybody knew by heart;
but one of them, not understanding,
tried to choose all three
and the older woman intervened
so the others took their turns.
Later we sat around dozing under pines
through part of the hot afternoon before
jumping up for horseshoes and dips in the lake
and animated talk, all of us at once.
You remember, this was all
so much like the other years,
and if I seem distant as I tell it now,
it is because of what happened next.

We walked back to the hall for dinner,
a nut roast, corn on cob, potatoes, gravy,
ice cream, your best recipe for every dish,
naturally the special punch, glass after glass.
While we shared our pleasure in this feast,
one of the youngest children started singing
unselfconsciously about a gray squirrel
with its acorn; then somebody else
in a voice we barely heard at first
began a second song, and the next moment
everyone all ages had joined in,

song after song after song unprompted,
and the melodies transported us
so that with no one leading we all stood and slowly
moved together, singing still, out on the deck
that was large enough to hold us all and where
we could see the lake, now darkening,
through the gaps between the pines,
likewise the stars overhead through branches;
and forgetting any plans we'd made,
went on, singing each new song,
whatever it was, in unison,
no one calling it, everyone feeling the same tune –
music of the beauty in a soul,
or sometimes of the silliness of souls,
so that we laughed softly, young and old,
and went on to sing about belonging to this place
that belonged to us
that belonged together while we sang.

We were all part of the lyrics
with the duck in a puddle, and
with the nightingale near the woods,
under the thousand stars in the skies,
and what was left after the ball was over,
Doctor John and his cod liver oil,
the drunken sailor with shaved belly,
and the swiftly flowing waters I believed
were home to tribes on the American plains
until the line about the castle in Hungary.

And the songs of heart and soul and of writing
oneself a letter, Remember the time you've had here,
and that no man is an island, unlike this night.

Oh it had a calendar date, but was it just
the year you missed and not some other life
belonging to greater distances than we have yet traveled,
a key far out of time hanging in midair

where the song wafted like misted nectar
that draws hummingbirds of any age and place?

Well, when we'd sung all the harmonies we knew,
all you'd ever taught us, our last notes
went off to live in the same night sky
that you might have been reflecting on,
while we sat silently lost in our thoughts
of one another sensing what had come to pass.

In our silence every now and then
we could hear boats chugging softly on the water,
then we drifted away like the melodies,
each of us to a separate place for the rest
of the night, linked in spirit yet aware
we could never truly hold this night
that would never let us go.

So I took my last drink of the evening,
cool mountain water from the oldest
fountain on the grounds, and then went back
to the hall where I found something else
of yours, the book of your knowledge,
the songs you led us in till they were second nature.
If I could, I knew that I must find you soon,
to return it, saying, Something of you
was there with us, your name written
on the inside cover, yes I know your hand.

❁

Passages

In a dream I see you
in the air above
as though from another sphere
radiant smile cheering me
in this empty room
while the book between my hands
is reeling, pages crackling
and spilling its alphabet
into my heart
there to shape new languages
of the lands we were to travel in,
walking there many a mile beyond
where I might be were it not
for you always before me
and with still unspoken words
to guide us.

❁

To Someone

People speak of their lives' twisted paths
that have led them where they are today
their vision dimming their walk hesitant
as if they'd known that it would come to this

every day your steps have brought you here
with the animal gladness of a child
where the trees have stood since before your time
you had no notion of their ancestry
it brought them joy to be loved for themselves

and you ask yourself as if for the moment
no one was trying to overhear
are you older than these trees that greet you
just as they have since you found them here

you were certain and they were certain
they would be there you would ride their branches
gracefully how could it be a question of age.

❁

Sharing Birthdays

But I cannot say with whom
and give away what I never owned
and our stars will wander anyway.

We were out one night to gaze at them
and because suddenly it was true
I told my friend I felt blessed.
They had done it with their light
trickling down to us.
It made him twinkle
and I knew he heard
though he said nothing
and we walked on anyway

into a time of extra fortune
but now it was the tested,
the downspinning kind
for the trial-size boats
we launched from a slipway to the sea
and because slowly it had come true
I murmured I no longer felt blessed.

But there was no one
to share reflections,
so I sailed on anyway

and looked up again
at the stars, we all did then,
believing they honored birthdays,
like distant candles,
blessing us anew,
and if they did not
then it was too soon to ask,
that first we'd have some other
assignment from those
busybodies in the sky,
guiding lights even while they follow
one another in their rounds,
too taken up like Archimedes
to smile on the parabolas
they can make of us.

What, is the answer
here alone, today?
Should I have known it all
before when it would have been
far more clear than it is now?

No, that isn't my story,
it's about the one I told
and who kept walking.
One day he'll return,
no more shining man,
and I'll say to you,
whose name I can tell
whenever you like,
Come on over, here's someone
I want you to meet.

❋

Pillar of Saint Gregorius

From our place in line we cannot see
those who came before yet they are here
in their viewless centuries
unlooked for thumbs hollowing out stone
one particle at a time
from this pillar of Gregorius
this was all we ever knew of them
so many and so long ago we living now
see no trace of them
but this tiny space

neither can they see us as
we press our thumbs over theirs
with a clockwise twist
sending strength and joy
onward to those we came to care for
like those before us
those who loved us that had yet to be

afterwards when we have sought our homes
in the still night the quiet hollow
alone hears the clock that tells
this hour each night every age.

❖

The Quiet Time

Earth sleeps too, while her trees
overwinter and build
strength to send their new leaves
to meet the wind come spring.

The snow spirit covers
her with a white blanket
thick enough to quiet
sounds that intrude on rest.

You know someone's taking
steps that you cannot hear,
but you turn under your
covers and think of the
stories you will whisper
tonight by crackling logs.

First ask silent blessing;
give thanks for the spirit
above ground, under sky,
whose strides are triply hushed,
by dream, by dream of snow,
by season's velvet glide.

A Christmas Prayer

Let every creature close its eyes
and find its peace tonight.
Let birds and bats and squirrels rest
without the need for flight.

Elk reposing, possums drifting,
even hawks must doze.
Many a night is plagued with ambush;
this is not one of those.

When all is calm I look to you,
your radiant eyes, your smile.
Come join me in the silent hours
and vigil keep some while.